Books should be returned or renewed by the last date above. Renew by phone **03000 41 31 31** or online *www.kent.gov.uk/libs*

C334428507

D1355302

TALES of AMAZING ANiMAL HEROES

REAL-LIFE STORIES OF ANIMAL BRAVERY

MIKE UNWIN

PUFFIN

THIS BOOK IS FOR ALL THOSE MEN
AND WOMEN IN TIMES OF WAR, PAST
AND PRESENT, WHO HAVE HAD THE
CONSCIENCE AND COURAGE TO
CARE FOR ANIMALS

MIKE UNWIN

INTRODUCTION

It's strange that it sometimes takes war to remind us that all of us, all the creatures of the earth, are one immense family. We are companions in this life, often relying on one another for survival, for comfort. We live alongside each other, breathe the same air, look up at the same skies, love our children, fight to survive. Animals feel pain and fear and hunger and loneliness as we do. They know trust and belonging and loyalty and affection as we do. They may not speak our languages, but they have their own way of talking. Listen to a blackbird in the garden – they have their own instincts, their own kind of intelligence, often superior to ours. Think of the journey of the swallow back home to England from Africa, thousands of miles over seas and mountains and deserts. And with no map, no sat nav . . . it's all in their bird-brain!

Read this wonderful book of stories of animal heroes, and we see that our fellow creatures are as remarkable as we are. Time and again in these tales, a horse, a dog, a bear, a goat, an elephant or a pig have shown us that animals, like us, can show great courage and immense loyalty, that they are the best and truest of companions. Time and again we see that, in the midst of the danger and horror of war, we and they have a common capacity for love.

I have written often about animals in my stories: horses, elephants, swallows, robins, polar bears, whales, narwhals, cats, dogs, chimpanzees, orangutans, wolves, tigers, lions, albatrosses, wombats – and all sorts of farm animals too. I have also written many books about animals in war.

What interests me in all my books about animals, and animals in war, is the friendship between us. How we rely on one another, understand one another, how kind we can be to them, and they to us, but also how cruel and exploitative we can be towards them.

We should remember that animals rely on us to look after our shared planet. To read this book is to understand how brave, loyal and loving animals can be. We need to repay that love. War does not only destroy people and animals, it also pollutes the planet, the habitat they need if they are to survive. In war and in peace we must never take our animal friends for granted.

As I write this, we are still making war on their seas, their rivers, cutting down their trees, occupying their land, driving them out – and, to our shame, we are still hunting some animals to extinction. Is that any way to treat our friends, our fellow creatures? Read this book and we know the answer.

Michael Morpurgo

CONTENTS

BUCEPHALUS

A HORSE MADE FOR GREATNESS

It was a terrifying sight for any horse. A line of trumpeting elephants thundered forward, their huge tusks gleaming. Arrows rained down from the archers mounted on their backs. And behind them came thousands of charging soldiers, brandishing their swords and shouting fierce battle cries.

But this was not any horse: it was the mighty black stallion Bucephalus. And proudly sitting on his sturdy back was Alexander the Great, ruler of Ancient Greece. Together, the two had seen many battles. Now, in the year 326 BC, Alexander's troops were facing the Indian army at the Battle of the Hydaspes.

Bucephalus's name means 'bull's head' in Ancient Greek – and this big horse was certainly as strong and proud as a bull. For many years, nobody had been able to tame him. When a horse trader tried to sell him to King Phillip the Second, Alexander's father, the King refused to buy him. He didn't want a horse that nobody could handle.

But young Alexander, who was only 13 years old, stepped forward. He spoke softly to Bucephalus and laid his cloak on the ground. He saw that the horse was alarmed by his own shadow – so he turned him to face the sun, leaving the shadow behind and out of sight. The young stallion quickly calmed down – Alexander had tamed him.

Phillip was amazed! He believed this was a sign that Alexander would grow up to be a great leader, and from that day Alexander and Bucephalus were inseparable. In 336 BC, after his father's death, Alexander took the throne. Together he and Bucephalus travelled far and wide, fighting battles and conquering distant lands in the name of the Greek Empire.

The Battle of the Hydaspes was Bucephalus's last. We can't be sure what happened: was Bucephalus killed in the fighting or did he simply die of old age? Either way, Alexander was devastated by the loss of his friend. He ordered the city of Bucephala to be built in the horse's honour, beside the Hydaspes River.

Today this river is called the Jhelum and it flows through Pakistan's Punjab province. There are no signs of the ancient city – but some believe that its ruins lie beneath the present-day town of Jalalpur Sharif. And perhaps, buried with them, are the bones of a noble horse.

HANNIBAL

AND THE MOUNTAIN-CLIMBING ELEPHANTS

The elephant tossed its head and trumpeted in alarm. The soldiers on its broad back clung on for dear life. No wonder the huge beast was so frightened: the narrow, rocky path ahead disappeared over a sheer cliff face. One more step and they would all have tumbled over the edge. Snow swirled around them as the mahout (keeper of the elephant) tried to calm the frightened animal. They would have to find another way down the mountain.

ONE MORE STEP AND THEY WOULD ALL HAVE TUMBLED OVER THE EDGE

A snowy mountainside is a strange place for elephants, who come from hot tropical places, such as Africa and India. But more than 2,000 years ago – in 218 AD – the great leader Hannibal led a team of 38 elephants over the Alps (a rugged mountain range in central Europe). Marching behind them was a

massive army: 38,000 foot soldiers and 8,000 men on horseback. It was a terrifying sight.

Hannibal was the general of Carthage, a great state in northern Africa. He was marching his army into Italy to fight the Romans – but he was taking a sneaky route through the mountains. He hoped this would surprise the Romans, and then his elephants would help him to defeat them. It was a clever plan. But winter was coming, and the conditions were very hard for the soldiers and animals.

Hannibal was not the first leader to use war elephants. In places such as ancient India and Persia, armies had fought with elephants for over a thousand years. The huge animals could trample enemies underfoot and scatter soldiers with their terrifying noise. Some wore metal armour to protect their foreheads, and soldiers rode on a special platform on their back, called a howdah, from where they fired arrows and had a better view of the battle. When the elephants were not in battle, they did lots of other hard work, such as carrying heavy equipment.

Hannibal's elephants struggled in the Alps. They were not used to the freezing cold weather, they couldn't find enough food, and the steep mountain paths were often too narrow for them. Many died. But they worked hard for Hannibal and his army, and helped them defeat the Romans in many famous battles across Europe.

GENGHIS KHAN

AND THE HARDY HORSES OF ANCIENT MONGOLIA

The horses galloped faster and faster, drumming up a cloud of dust across the wide, empty plains. On their backs rode the archers, with their bows raised, ready to fire. They had been riding for many days and now their enemies were close. They drove their horses forward, clinging on with perfect balance as they prepared to attack.

Eight hundred years ago, during the 13th century AD, Mongolia had the largest empire the world has ever known. It stretched from Europe in the west right across to the sea of Japan in the east. How did the Mongolians build such a mighty empire? 'It is easy to conquer the world from the back of a horse,' said Genghis Khan, their ruler.

The people of Mongolia are among the best horse riders in the world. They say that a Mongolian without a horse is like a bird without wings. Every family member has his or her own horse, and children learn to ride when they are just three years old.

It's no wonder, then, that horses were so important to the Mongolian army! They could carry soldiers for thousands of miles, and gallop across deserts taking messages from one remote outpost to another.

Mongolian horses are not like the horses in Europe or America. They are smaller, but they are very tough and strong. They do not need stables, because they live wild on the open plains, called steppes, where they find their own food – even digging through the snow during winter. They can survive in all kinds of weather and have incredible powers of endurance.

The riders of ancient Mongolia also had special skills, which they had learned as hunters. They could fire their arrows while riding at full tilt, or slide down one flank of their galloping horse to avoid enemies on the other side. Life was hard and battles were brutal, but the soldiers always treated their horses kindly. Unlike riders elsewhere, they did not use sharp spurs on their boots, and Genghis Khan declared it a crime to strike a horse. Before a battle, soldiers sprinkled mare's milk on the ground for good luck.

In Mongolia today, horses are still very important. There are more than three million in the country – that's roughly one for every person. And you can still see the dust rising over the wide plains, as riders gallop like the wind.

MURPHY

THE STRETCHER-BEARER DONKEY

Slowly but surely, the donkey picked his way down the rocky gully. On his back was a wounded soldier, one arm draped around another soldier walking alongside him. A machine gun rattled and bullets whizzed past like angry wasps. But the donkey didn't falter. He continued his careful journey, placing one hoof in front of another.

The donkey was called Murphy and the soldier walking beside him was Private John Simpson Kirkpatrick, known to his friends as Simpson. It was April 1915. British and French troops, alongside soldiers from Australia and New Zealand (together known as Anzacs), had recently landed on the Turkish coast at a place called Gallipoli. They had planned to move inland and attack the enemy – but the enemy were fighting back. Now the Allied troops were trapped near the beaches where they had landed.

Private Simpson was a stretcher bearer for the Anzacs, so his job was to rescue wounded men and take them to the makeshift hospital. It was exhausting and dangerous work and sometimes it took three days just to bring back one soldier. When Simpson met Murphy, he had an idea. Perhaps a donkey could help . . .

Murphy came from the Greek island of Lemnos. More than 1,000 horses and donkeys had been brought to Gallipoli to help move heavy equipment. Donkeys are very strong, and Simpson soon found that Murphy made his job much easier. The two friends worked tirelessly from dawn to dusk, carrying injured soldiers from battlefield to beach. The troops cheered as they passed.

Around his head Murphy wore a white band with a red cross. This showed the enemy that he was a stretcher bearer, so they knew not to shoot at him or Simpson. Even so, the work was very dangerous. Simpson's luck finally ran out on 19 May, when he was killed by an enemy bullet while rescuing another injured soldier. Murphy was next to him as usual, but despite losing his friend, he continued the difficult journey, carrying the injured soldier all the way to the hospital. He saved the soldier's life.

Murphy's work didn't stop there, and he started work with another stretcher bearer called Dick Henderson. Later, he was adopted by a unit of Indian soldiers. After nearly 11 months of fighting at Gallipoli, the battle ended. Nobody knows what happened to Murphy. But in 1997 he was posthumously awarded the Purple Cross for outstanding animal bravery in battle.

CHER AMI

THE MAJOR'S LAST HOPE

Bang! Bang! Shots rang out as the pigeon took flight. She flapped fast, twisting and turning – but too late, she was hit. Down she plummeted, into the bushes. And then, to the soldiers' amazement, she took off again. This time she dodged the bullets. Zigzagging at lightning speed, she disappeared towards the horizon.

The pigeon's name was Cher Ami, which means 'dear friend' in French. She had been donated to a battalion of American soldiers based in northern France during the First World War. It was 3 October 1918, near the end of the War, and the battalion had been trapped in a forest by the German army.

Major Charles Whittlesey was in charge and he was desperate for help. Only 194 men were left – caught between the German army and the firing of their own side, who didn't know they were there. The major had sent out messengers for help, but all had been shot or captured. Desperate now, he decided to send a note by pigeon.

The first pigeon was shot down. So was the second. Cher Ami was the major's last hope. He fitted a small note inside a canister on her leg. It said: 'We are along the road parallel [to] 276.4. Our own artillery is dropping a barrage directly on us. For heavens' sake stop it.' Then he released her.

Thousands of pigeons were used by the British forces during the War. Often, these fast-flying birds were the only way to get an important message through. Soon the Germans began shooting down every pigeon they saw – but Cher Ami was no ordinary pigeon. She had delivered 12 messages before, and this time she was determined to succeed again.

Despite being hit, Cher Ami flew on, reaching headquarters 40 kilometres away in just 25 minutes. She was badly injured: shot through the breast, blinded in one eye and with one leg almost lost. Nonetheless, she had made it. The soldiers at headquarters read her message, and immediately set out to rescue Major Whittlesey and his battalion. One plucky pigeon had saved 195 lives.

Back at base, the medics worked hard to save the life of the brave bird. They treated her wounds and even made a tiny wooden leg to replace her injured one. Once she was well enough to travel, she sailed to the USA, where she was welcomed as a hero. Before her death, on 13 June 1919, Cher Ami received many awards for her bravery, including a special French wartime medal called the Croix de Guerre.

WARRIOR

THE HORSE WHO LED THE CHARGE

The magnificent horse galloped forward into the sparse wood. Bullets whizzed past, thudding into tree trunks and cutting down other horses galloping alongside him. Shells whined and exploded, machine guns rattled and injured men cried out in pain. The noise and smoke were terrifying. But the horse didn't waver. He pressed on, carrying his rider into the heat of battle.

Warrior, the perfect name for this mighty horse, was a thoroughbred. A fine chestnut stallion, he was born on the Isle of Wight in 1908. His owner, Jack Seely, was also from a distinguished family, and a close friend of Winston Churchill, who would one day become Prime Minister of Great Britain. Jack had grown up with Warrior – so when the First World War broke out, he took his loyal horse to fight with him. Together they arrived in France on 11 August 1914.

Now it was 30 March 1918, four years later, and the daring duo were riding together into battle for the last time.

THE NOISE AND SMOKE WERE TERRIFYING

The War was drawing to an end and the German army had recently launched its final offensive, pushing forward with thousands of men. In northern France, in a place called Moreuil Wood, the Allied troops were fighting back. Jack Seely was now commander of the Canadian Cavalry Brigade. He led the charge, as usual, mounted on Warrior. Whatever happened, he knew his trusty horse would not let him down.

Danger was nothing new to Warrior. He had galloped into action on the very first day of the Battle of the Somme, a 141-day battle in which nearly one million men were either wounded or killed. There had been many other narrow escapes. At the Battle of Passchendaele, soldiers had dug him out of deep mud, after he was buried when a shell exploded nearby. And twice he had escaped in the nick of time as the burning beams of his stable roof collapsed around him. He had suffered many injuries – and yet, miraculously, he had always managed to survive.

No wonder the soldiers loved Warrior and patted his flanks whenever they passed him. To them, this big, handsome

horse was a lucky charm. What's more, he never showed a glimmer of fear. Unsurprisingly, war is a traumatic experience for most animals: the terrifying noises and strange smells usually send them running away in fear. Yet Warrior would stand calm and still as shells exploded around him and bullets whistled overhead. And Seely usually rode at the head of the column, so he and Warrior were first in the line of fire. The horse's bravery gave the soldiers extra courage to face the terrors of the War.

The Germans were eventually defeated at the Battle of Moreuil Wood and this marked a turning point in the War. Then, in November 1918, the War finally came to an end. Warrior had survived. He returned with his owner to the Isle of Wight, where he was hailed as a hero. Jack Seely, who was now a general, continued to look after his trusty horse. Despite the injuries Warrior had suffered, he was still a horse that loved to gallop. On 30 March 1922 - exactly four years to the day since he had led the charge at the Battle of Moreuil Wood – he won a famous point-to-point race across the island.

Warrior died in 1941 at the ripe old age of 33. His obituary was written in *The Times* newspaper – something that was unheard of for an animal. Jack Seely wrote a book about his famous horse, and in 2014 Warrior was awarded the PDSA Dickin Medal, the highest military award an animal can receive.

SERGEANT BILL

THE HEAD-BUTTING GOAT

Bump! Biff! Bash! One by one, the goat butted the three soldiers off their feet, knocking them into the trench. Sprawling in the mud, the men wondered what on earth the animal was doing. But before they could get up, a huge explosion rang out. A shell had landed where they had been standing seconds earlier. The goat must have heard it coming before they did. This plucky animal had just saved their lives.

The amazing story of Sergeant Bill began in Canada, on 23 August 1914. A train taking Canadian soldiers to fight stopped at a small town called Boardview. The soldiers spied a handsome goat pulling a cart along beside the tracks. They persuaded his owner, a young girl called Daisy Curwain, to let them take him along as a lucky mascot.

Soldiers were not supposed to take mascots to war but these Canadians had grown very attached to Bill and they smuggled him on to the train inside an empty orange crate. Soon they had got him aboard a ship and were sailing across the Atlantic to England, where their battle training started. In February 1915, the soldiers received their orders to proceed to the front line in France. Of course, they took Bill with them.

At the front, Bill could be a real nuisance. He nosed around the soldier's quarters, nibbling anything he could find and even drinking beer from the canteen! Twice he was arrested: once for chewing up some important documents and once for charging an officer.

But nobody minded Bill's antics. After all, this brave goat had saved three soldiers' lives. In many fierce battles, he stood beside his human companions. Once he even helped guard a prisoner trapped in a shell crater. Like the soldiers, he endured all the discomforts of war, including gas, trench foot and shell shock, and twice he was wounded by shrapnel. But he was always with the troops, keeping their spirits up. The men so admired Bill that in February 1915 they gave him the honorary rank of sergeant.

Despite his injuries, Sergeant Bill survived the War. When peace was declared, he returned to Canada, where he marched with his men in a grand victory parade, wearing a special blue coat with sergeant's stripes. The soldiers returned him to his original owner, Daisy Curwain, who looked after him for the rest of his days.

Bill received many awards for his bravery, including the 1914/1915 Star, the British War Medal and the Victory Medal. Today you can see him stuffed and mounted in the Broadview Museum, looking as brave and defiant as ever.

STUBBY

THE SALUTING SUPERDOG

Woof, woof, woof! The urgent bark of a dog rang out along the trench. Corporal Robert Conroy knew exactly what this meant. 'Gas!' he shouted to the men around him. 'Stubby can smell it. Quick!'

Just in time, the soldiers grabbed their gas masks and pulled them tight over their faces. Then, as Stubby came running up to them, they fitted him with his own mask. Seconds later, the deadly gas cloud came rolling across the edge of the trench where they were crouching. But behind their masks, the soldiers could breathe safely.

Stubby wasn't very big. A mongrel, he stood just 40cm (16 inches) tall. Like all dogs, though, he had an excellent sense of smell. For the men of the US 102nd Infantry Regiment, fighting on the Western Front in 1918, this was a lifesaver. Stubby's sharp nose detected the scent of deadly mustard gas long before the soldiers could, and his barking raised the alarm.

Smell wasn't Stubby's only superpower. His sensitive hearing also meant that he could hear the high-pitched whine of shells overhead – long before any human could. His warning barks gave his human companions a chance to take cover. And when the men were creeping towards the German lines, Stubby used his sharp eyesight to look for lurking enemy soldiers. If he saw one, he would wag his tail, silently warning his companions without giving away their position.

Stubby wasn't born an army dog. In fact, nobody knew exactly where he came from! Back in the USA, he had simply appeared one day in the grounds of Yale University, while the men of the 102nd Regiment were doing their military training. The soldiers were amused by the funny little dog that hung around to watch them. Soon they adopted him as their mascot, calling him Stubby because of his short tail. One soldier, Corporal Conroy, became particularly fond of him, and used to give him treats and teach him tricks.

In 1917, the 102nd Regiment was posted to France to fight on the Western Front. Corporal Conroy didn't want to leave Stubby behind, so he smuggled him aboard the ship. As the regiment was disembarking at the end of their voyage, the commanding officer spotted something wriggling under Conroy's overcoat. When the embarrassed soldier released Stubby and set him down, the clever dog

saluted the officer with his paw – just like his master had taught him. The officer was so impressed that he allowed the regiment to keep their dog.

Stubby served on the front line for eight months: during that time, he survived 17 battles. Not only did he help save his companions from poison gas attacks and shell fire, he also helped locate wounded soldiers who were lying out in no man's land. Once he even captured an enemy spy, holding him by his trousers until the soldiers could arrive and arrest him. In turn, the soldiers made the dog his own special gas mask to help keep him safe alongside them.

HE COMFORTED THEM THROUGH ALL THE TERROR AND HARDSHIP

The men loved their brave mascot, he cheered them up and comforted them through all the terror and hardship of the War. When Corporal Conroy was injured, Stubby accompanied his master to the hospital, where he wandered about, greeting and entertaining the other injured men. And when Stubby himself was wounded – hit in the chest and leg by shrapnel from an exploding German

grenade – he was treated in the soldiers' hospital rather than the animal hospital.

Stubby's heroic deeds saw him promoted unofficially to the rank of sergeant, and he received numerous medals, including the Purple Heart. After Stubby helped his regiment rescue the French village of Château-Thierry from the German army, some villagers made him a special jacket from chamois. Now he could trot around proudly with his medals pinned to his coat for all to admire.

When Corporal Conroy brought Stubby back to America after the War, the dog was celebrated as a famous war hero. He met three American presidents – Woodrow Wilson, Warren Harding and Calvin Coolidge. He also became a mascot for a basketball team called the Georgetown Hoyas, and used to entertain the crowd by pushing the ball around the court at half-time. After he died peacefully in 1926, *The New York Times* newspaper published a special obituary, and in 2018 Stubby became famous all over again when a special film about his life entertained cinema-goers around the world.

LIZZIE

THE HIGH-STREET ELEPHANT

On a cold, grey day in the northern English town of Sheffield, a big, grey elephant came lumbering down the cobbled street. Her trunk swung gently from side to side as she pulled her heavy load of scrap metal. In most towns, people would have stopped to stare. But the residents of Sheffield had grown used to Lizzie the elephant and they waved as the friendly beast passed by. They knew she had a job to do.

It was 1916, the middle of the First World War. Sheffield was very important to Britain's war effort because its factories produced steel for making machinery and weapons. Much of this steel came from melting down old iron that scrap metal dealers collected around town. But now there was a problem: many of the scrap dealers' working horses had been sent away to help the soldiers in France. It was becoming difficult to transport the heavy loads to the factories.

Lizzie came to the rescue. Before the War, she had been part of a travelling animal

menagerie so she was used to working with people. What's more, she was strong enough to do the work of three horses. A scrap metal dealer called Tommy Ward borrowed her from the menagerie. He fitted her with a harness and made her special leather boots to protect her feet from the metal rubbish around the scrap yard. Soon Lizzie was hauling her heavy loads around Sheffield. Thanks to her, the factories could continue to make steel.

Lizzie became a celebrity around Sheffield. Everybody loved to see her ambling down their street! She was not only a hard worker but also an entertaining personality. There are many

stories about what she got up to: some say she once reached her trunk through a kitchen window and stole a pie; others that she ate a schoolboy's cap.

We are not sure what happened to Lizzie after the War – she may have continued working for Tommy Ward, or she may have returned to the menagerie. She may even have gone to work on a farm, where the ground was softer on her feet. What we do know is that she captured the hearts of the people of Sheffield during the dark days of the War and today she is still remembered in the city.

TIRPITZ

THE SHIPWRECKED PIG

'What's that?' shouted the sailor, peering out from the deck of HMS *Glasgow*. 'It looks like a pig!' said his companion. The two of them squinted across the waves. There – amid bits of floating wreckage from the sinking German ship – they could see two pink ears and a round snout bobbing above the surface. Sure enough, it was a pig. And it was swimming straight towards them. The two men stripped off their jackets and prepared to dive into the sea.

The ship slowly slipping beneath the Pacific Ocean was the German cruiser SMS *Dresden*. It had been looking for a safe harbour near Robinson Crusoe Island, off the coast of South America. But, unable to escape from the guns of the British fleet, the captain had decided to sink his own vessel. The crew rowed ashore in lifeboats, leaving most of their equipment and possessions behind. Among these were many animals that they had been carrying as supplies. Most drowned – but one pig had managed to make her way above deck and escape.

The sailors had quite a struggle rescuing the battling pig. Eventually, with the help of a winch, they managed to get her aboard HMS *Glasgow*. The crew was very impressed by how this plucky animal had stayed on board the sinking ship after her shipmates had left and they decided to adopt her as the ship mascot. They named her Tirpitz, after Alfred von Tirpitz, the admiral of the German navy. As a joke, they even awarded her the Iron Cross, the top German military medal for bravery.

Tirpitz remained on board HMS *Glasgow* for a year, cheering up the sailors during their long, hard days at sea. In 1916 she returned to England, where she found a new home at Whale Island Gunnery School in Portsmouth. Here she joined many other animals, including chickens, geese and even wallabies. Her big appetite made her a bit of a nuisance: she was often breaking into chicken runs to steal their food.

Eventually Tirpitz ended up back with Captain John Luce, the former commander of HMS *Glasgow*. In 1917, she was bought by the 6th Duke of Portland in an auction to raise money for the Red Cross. We don't know what happened to her after that. But today, at the Imperial War Museum in London, you can see her stuffed head and a pair of silver mounted carvers made from her trotters – reminders of a day when she was a sailor on the ocean wave.

ROB

THE PARACHUTING DOG

Monday 22 January 1945 was a proud day for the owners of Rob, a Border collie from Shropshire. Rob had just won the Dickin Medal for his work as a patrol and guard dog – and for making an astonishing 20 parachute jumps.

Imagine a dog making 20 parachute jumps! No wonder Rob received his award. The missions had been very secret. It was said they took place at night and that Rob wore black make-up to camouflage his white patches. When he landed he would go ahead of the soldiers and signal when the enemy were close. He even helped rescue prisoners of war from behind enemy lines.

After Rob died, in 1952, his owners built a stone memorial on their family farm. In the years that followed, his fame grew: a book was written about him, and in 2004 Princess Anne unveiled a statue of him – and other animal war heroes – in Park Lane, London.

It's an amazing story. But is it true? In 2006 a soldier called Jimmy Quentin Hughes told a very different story. Jimmy had belonged to Rob's SAS regiment in Italy. And according to him, Rob had never made a parachute jump. In reality, the dog had been well-loved by his regiment, but after a while his owners had asked the regiment to give him back. The men didn't want to lose him, so they hatched a plan to convince the owners that Rob's work was so important he would have to stay. And what could be more impressive than a frequently parachute-jumping dog?

In fact, the men *had* tried to make a parachute jump with Rob. Windy weather had forced them to cancel the flight but they decided to pretend that it had happened anyway, and wrote to tell the owners all about it. Their plan worked! Rob stayed with the regiment for the rest of the War.

By the time Jimmy Hughes's story came to light, Rob had already passed away. We may never know the truth, but what we do know is that Rob really did serve with the SAS in North Africa and Italy, and he really did work as a guard dog behind enemy lines. We also know that other dogs have made parachute jumps, so Rob's adventures would not have been impossible.

Many strange and confusing things happen in wartime and it is sometimes hard to separate fact from fiction. Whatever the truth about Rob the para-dog, he certainly inspired brave soldiers during a terrible time. And isn't that worth a medal?

MARY

THE SHOEMAKER'S SAVIOUR PIGEON

Whoosh! The pigeon could hear the hawk zooming in behind her, getting closer. At the last second, she changed direction. The fierce bird of prey shot past, its deadly talons clutching at thin air. Missed! The pigeon redoubled her speed, flapping even faster, and soon left the hawk behind. Once more, she had managed to escape.

Some say that cats have nine lives. Perhaps pigeons have even more! During World War Two, a pigeon called Mary of Exeter survived numerous brushes with death. Carrying vital wartime messages back to England from the Allied troops in France, this brave bird was often targeted by German hawks, which had been trained to hunt carrier pigeons. She also avoided bullets and bombs, and even managed to escape when the German air force bombed her home town of Exeter, destroying her pigeon loft and killing many other pigeons.

Mary did not always get away unharmed, though. Once, a hawk almost caught her,

leaving nasty claw wounds on her neck and breast before she slipped free. On other occasions she was hit by shrapnel and even had the end of one wing shot off. But each time the brave bird recovered, passed her flying tests and returned to her daring, dangerous work.

Mary's owner was Charlie Brewer, a shoemaker from Exeter, in south-west England, who also worked as an intelligence agent during the War. Charlie used his skills with needle and thread to stitch up Mary's wounds and remove pellets from her body. Once he even made a special leather collar to help her hold her head up after her neck was injured.

Pigeons played a vital role during World

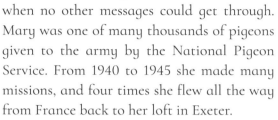

War Two, often carrying top secret information from behind enemy lines when no other messages could get through. Mary was one of many thousands of pigeons given to the army by the National Pigeon Service. From 1940 to 1945 she made many missions, and four times she flew all the way from France back to her loft in Exeter.

Mary died in 1950, and today a blue plaque in Exeter shows where, for 63 years, Charlie Brewer lived and ran his shoemaker's business. This was also where he bred and trained his pigeons, and it was the home of Mary, whose amazing escapes made her the talk of the town.

CHIPS

THE SPIRITED SENTRY DOG

As dawn broke over the island of Sicily, the American soldiers of the 3rd Infantry Division found themselves trapped on the beach. They had waded ashore from the landing craft, ready to advance inland. But now they could go no further. An enemy machine-gunner, hidden in a hut at the top of the beach, fired constant bursts of deadly gunfire. The soldiers kept their heads down and wondered what to do.

Chips was having none of it. This trained sentry dog had landed with the soldiers and was growing impatient. Suddenly he broke free from his handler, Private John Rowell, and raced up the beach towards the hut. Bullets rattled past but the dog moved like lightning. Within seconds he had reached the hut and burst inside.

The US soldiers heard a shot ring out. They rushed after Chips, fearing the worst. But the next thing they saw was an enemy soldier struggling outside, with Chips' jaws fastened firmly around him. Four more enemy soldiers followed close behind, their hands raised in surrender. Chips had captured the gun emplacement single-handed.

The brave dog was wounded during the fight – grazed by a bullet and scorched by close-range gunfire. But his heroics were not over for the day. That evening, his keen nose helped his human companions detect and capture ten hidden enemy soldiers further inland. Now, thanks to Chips, the soldiers of the 3rd Infantry could continue on their mission.

Chips was born in New York state, USA. A big, handsome dog, and the terror of local postmen, he was part collie, part German shepherd and part husky. In 1942, his owner Edward Wren donated him to the US army, who trained Chips as a sentry dog. Chips then joined the 3rd Infantry Division on their missions in Europe and North Africa. (By coincidence, the Allied invasion of Sicily, in which Chips served, was code-named Operation Husky.)

This dependable dog met many important people. He worked as a sentry at a war conference in Casablanca, Morocco, where US president Franklin D. Roosevelt met British prime minister Winston Churchill. And he once bit American general Dwight D. Eisenhower – just because he was trained to bite any stranger who tried to pet him.

After the War, Chips returned to live with his owner in New York state. Sadly, he died in 1946, one year later, having never recovered fully from the wounds he received in action. During his lifetime, Chips received many unofficial medals – and in 2018, 72 years after his death, he was awarded the PDSA Dickin Medal for animal bravery.

GANDER

THE DOG WHO INSPIRED A LEGEND

The Japanese soldiers froze. They could hear a low rumbling growl ahead. Suddenly a big, black shape came tearing out of the darkness. Could this be the legendary 'black beast' that roamed Hong Kong Island? Terrified, they turned and ran. Too late: the beast was soon snapping at their heels, growling and snarling savagely.

In reality, there was no mythical monster. The 'black beast' was Gander, a big, shaggy Newfoundland dog. And behind him came the soldiers of the Canadian Royal Rifles, shouting and firing their guns. These soldiers were fighting alongside the British army, trying to prevent the Japanese army from invading Hong Kong, and Gander – their regimental mascot – was fighting by their side.

Gander came from the island of Newfoundland in Eastern Canada. Originally he belonged to the Hayden family, who named him Pal. Like all Newfoundland dogs, he was big and strong, and he used to pull the children through the snow on a sledge. But one day he accidentally scratched one of the children. The family were worried that he might be trouble, so they gave him to the nearby army base, where he was renamed Gander, after a local town.

The soldiers of the Canadian Royal Rifles loved Gander. They let him march at the head of the battalion and took him with them when they sailed to Hong Kong. Rifleman Ted Kelly was assigned to look after Gander, and used to give the dog an occasional tot of beer as a treat. In Hong Kong, Gander took long cold showers to escape from the baking heat – which, being a dog from the cold north, he wasn't used to.

The battle of Hong Kong lasted from 8–25 December 1941. The fighting was fierce and many soldiers died on both sides. Eventually the Japanese took control of the island and the Allied forces surrendered. On three occasions, Gander helped fight and the Japanese became convinced that the Allies were training special ferocious animals for battle. The third time, sadly, was the last. Gander grabbed a Japanese grenade in his jaws and carried it away from his regiment. The grenade exploded, killing the brave dog – but not before he had saved the lives of seven wounded Canadian soldiers.

In October 2000 Gander was posthumously awarded the PDSA Dickin Medal for his brave deeds. It was the first Dickin Medal issued to an animal for over 50 years.

SIMON

THE CHAMPION RAT-CATCHER

When Lieutenant Commander Bernard Skinner entered his cabin, he found a nasty surprise. There, on the foot of his bed, was a large dead rat. As commander of the British naval frigate HMS *Amethyst*, the captain wasn't easily shocked, but he certainly wasn't expecting this. It must be a 'gift' from Simon the cat, he realized. Sure enough, he soon spied the culprit, snugly curled up inside his gold-braided cap.

Luckily, Bernard Skinner liked cats. What's more, he knew just what an important job Simon was doing. Rats were a problem on ships, spreading disease and nibbling food supplies. HMS *Amethyst* was docked in Hong Kong. It was 1949 and the ship had been sent to keep order during the civil war in nearby mainland China.

Simon had been wandering the docks when one of the sailors found him and smuggled him aboard the *Amethyst*. The hungry cat wasted no time hunting down the rodents hiding around the ship. He soon became very popular with the crew, who gave him his name and taught him tricks, such as fishing ice cubes from a jug of water.

In April, disaster struck. HMS *Amethyst* sailed on a mission up the Yangtze River to the Chinese town of Nanjing. Along the way, the ship came under attack from the Chinese rebel army. After a barrage of gunfire, 56 members of the ship's crew lay dead or wounded. Bernard Skinner was killed and Simon was missing.

When Simon reappeared two days later, he was badly burned and injured by shrapnel. The crew feared the worst, but to their amazement the plucky cat recovered. For the next three months, while HMS *Amethyst* remained on the river, Simon resumed his rat-catching duties. What's more, his friendly purr raised the spirits of the wounded men whenever he visited them in the sick bay.

By the time HMS *Amethyst* returned to the UK, Simon's story had spread. Many people wrote letters and sent gifts, and he was awarded the PDSA Dickin Medal for animal gallantry – the only one ever awarded to a cat.

Sadly, Simon never received his medal. Like all animals returning to Britain, he had to stay in quarantine for six months to avoid spreading a disease. During this time he developed a viral infection – probably from his injuries on the ship – and on 28 November 1949 he died. Hundreds of people attended his burial at Ilford Animal Cemetery, where there is a special monument in his memory.

WOJTEK

THE LOYAL SOLDIER BEAR

Beside a small railway station in the mountains of Persia (now Iran), a truck pulled over. A group of travelling refugees and soldiers clambered out. They had seen a young shepherd boy holding a wriggling sack, and were curious to find out what was inside. Besides, their journey had been long and tiring, and they needed a break.

The boy untied the sack and, to everyone's amazement, out tumbled a little furry bear cub. He explained that hunters had shot the mother bear, and now he was looking for someone to take care of the baby. The travellers were enchanted: many of them were also orphans because of the War. They took the bear from the boy in return for some chocolate and a penknife.

The date was 8 April 1942. The soldiers were Polish, and were on a long journey south from Russia, where – along with many others – they had been kept as prisoners of war. Now that Russia was at war with Germany, the soldiers

had been released and were returning to Europe to fight again. First they would travel to Egypt, to meet up with the British army.

The cub was skinny and underfed. He happily guzzled the condensed milk the soldiers fed him from a bottle. As their journey continued, passing through the deserts of Iraq and Palestine, the bear grew steadily bigger and stronger. He was a tame, confident little character. They soon fell in love with him, and named him Wojtek, which means 'happy fighter'.

By the time the soldiers reached Alexandria, in Egypt, Wojtek weighed over 200kg and stood 1.8 metres tall on his back legs. He was guzzling much more than milk now. Every morning he would amble over to the cookhouse for cereal, biscuits, bread, marmalade . . . and anything else he could scrounge. Fruit was a particular favourite – as was honey, which the men gave him from their own rations. He also loved beer and, being so big, he could drink plenty of it without getting drunk.

Sometimes though, Wojtek's appetite got him into trouble. Once he raided the camp food stores, tearing down shelves, spilling oil and generally making a terrible mess. He also stole clothes from washing lines, and worked out how to turn on the showers, quickly using up the soldiers' precious water rations.

But Wojtek was such great company that the soldiers forgave his bad behaviour. His playfulness kept their spirits up. What's more, he seemed to think he was one of them, riding in the truck, joining in their football matches and even learning to salute when greeted. He especially loved to wrestle with the soldiers, but despite his great strength, not to mention his sharp teeth and claws, he never harmed anyone.

THE SOLDIERS FORGAVE HIS BAD BEHAVIOUR

In Alexandria, the soldiers trained hard, and soon they were ready to return to the War as the 22nd Artillery Supply Company. In 1944 they were posted to Italy to help the Allied forces fight the Germans. But as they prepared to sail across the Mediterranean, they discovered animals were not allowed on the ship. Determined not to leave Wojtek behind, the soldiers drafted him as a private in the Polish army. He was now an official soldier, so he received his own serial number and paybook, and – most importantly – he was given double rations.

Once in Italy, the soldiers were soon in action. Wojtek proved to be very useful. With his great strength, he could shift 100kg crates of artillery shells, ready for the gunners to use. The big bear worked alongside the men during fierce fighting at the Battle of Monte Cassino. His legend spread and he became a firm favourite with visiting generals, who always asked to meet him.

Polish soldiers played an important role in the Second World War. Their pilots flew in the Battle of Britain and theirs was the first flag raised after victory in the Battle of Monte Cassino. For Polish people everywhere, Wojtek became a symbol of strength and pride. The new emblem of the company was a picture of a bear carrying a shell. After the War, the soldiers were unable to return to their homeland and were settled at an army base in Hutton, Scotland. Wojtek lived with them on camp until 1947, when the army was demobilized. With nowhere to go, he was taken to Edinburgh Zoo.

Wojtek never left the zoo. He died there in 1963 at the grand old bear age of 21, and although he was well cared for, he missed his old friends. When soldiers came to visit he always perked up, and he loved to hear people speaking Polish. Today there is a bronze statue of him in Krakow, Poland, and another in Edinburgh. Both are reminders of how much the British owed the people of Poland during the Second World War, and how much one friendly bear changed the lives of his soldiers.

JET

THE SEARCH-AND-RESCUE DOG

Jet refused to move. For nearly 12 hours the rescuers had been searching the rubble and pulling out the wounded. The German bombing raid had left the London hotel almost completely demolished, and now the rescuers were convinced that nobody was left inside. But Jet knew better. The rescue dog sat bolt upright, staring at the building, ears pricked. 'There's still somebody in there,' said his handler, Corporal Wardle. 'Jet's never wrong.'

Jet was right, of course. When the rescuers went back in for a final time they found a woman trapped inside the wreckage of the building. Amazingly, she was still alive. They managed to get her to safety and she went on to make a full recovery. Jet had saved yet another life.

Jet did not start out as a rescue dog. This handsome pedigree German shepherd was born in Liverpool in 1942, during the middle of the Second World War. He was soon sent to the War Dogs School in Gloucestershire, where he learned anti-sabotage work. For the next 18 months, Jet worked for the US army in Northern Ireland, checking that their airfields had not been sabotaged.

In 1944, however, the German air force renewed their bombing of London in a campaign known as

the 'Baby Blitz'. Jet was quickly retrained as a search-and-rescue dog, and went with Corporal Wardle to help the Civil Defence Forces of London. Wardle and Jet were the first to be used in official civil defence rescue duties.

Together, Jet and Corporal Wardle helped save the lives of more than 50 people trapped by the bombing. In January 1945, Jet was awarded the PDSA Dickin Medal for his hard work and bravery. When the War was over, Jet led the V-E (Victory in Europe) Day parade through London.

Jet's work didn't end with the armistice: in 1947 there was a disaster at William Pit, a coal mine in north-west England. A huge explosion had left many miners trapped underground and at the mercy of deadly poisonous gas. Jet was one of three dogs who were rushed to the scene, using their special skills to help rescue as many people as they could. For this heroic work, Jet received the RSPCA's Medallion of Valour.

Jet died in November 1949. A memorial was built for him in the English flower gardens at Calderstones Park in Liverpool, his home town. In 2016 local school children came to clean the memorial in a special service of remembrance.

WINKIE

THE PIGEON WHO CROSSED THE SEA

Four men crouched in a small rubber dinghy. They were wet, exhausted and chilled to the bone. Wreckage from their aircraft, an RAF Beaufort bomber, floated around them and the waves were slick with spilled oil. The men had managed to escape into their life raft before the plane sank. But now they were alone, surrounded by the sea.

It was 23 February 1942. The men had been returning to Scotland across the North Sea from a bombing mission in Norway, when their plane came under enemy fire.

Badly damaged, it was forced to ditch in the sea. Now the men were just 160 kilometres from home, but nobody knew they were there – and they had no radio to call for help. As their little boat bobbed in the waves, they feared the worst.

Little did they know, help was on its way. There had been one other passenger on the plane: a female blue-checkered pigeon, air force number NEHU 40 NSL. This plucky bird had escaped from her cage as the bomber began to sink.

Flapping as hard as she could, she had struggled free from the oily waves and taken to the air. Then she did exactly what homing pigeons do best: she headed for home.

Home was a pigeon loft in the village of Broughty Ferry, 190 kilometres away. The flight was exhausting: the bird was cold and wet, and her feathers were clogged with oil. But she battled on and finally she arrived. George Ross, the pigeon's owner, was very surprised to see his bird appear so late and so bedraggled. He knew she must have come from an aircraft. Many aircraft at that time carried pigeons, in case they were needed to send an emergency message.

George alerted the nearby RAF air base at Leuchars. They already knew that a plane had come down in the sea but they didn't

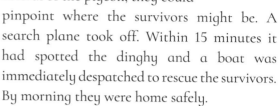

know where. Now, by working out the time difference between the bomber ditching and the arrival of the pigeon, they could pinpoint where the survivors might be. A search plane took off. Within 15 minutes it had spotted the dinghy and a boat was immediately despatched to rescue the survivors. By morning they were home safely.

The air base held a special dinner in the pigeon's honour. Throughout the evening, she perched in her cage, one eye blinking with exhaustion. Seeing this, the airmen called her Winkie. Now, at last, she had a name! The next year Winkie was awarded the Dickin Medal for animal bravery – one of the first ever to receive this honour.

BANDOOLA

THE ELEPHANT WHO LED THE ESCAPE

One more step and Bandoola had reached the top of the cliff. He heaved his huge body up on to the flat ground to find the other elephants waiting. Together, they had climbed nearly 100 metres and now they were finally safe. Birdsong drifted up from the jungle far below. It seemed another world away. 'Well done, boy!' said Elephant Bill, patting Bandoola's flanks. 'I knew you could make it.'

Elephant Bill's real name was Lieutenant Colonel James Howard Williams. He had always loved all kinds of animals, but his real favourites were elephants. In 1920, after serving in the First World War, Bill went to work in Burma (now Myanmar). Here, elephants carried logs from the timber plantations and did lots of other heavy lifting work. Bill travelled around this hot, tropical country, looking after elephants and learning how to train them. He soon became an elephant expert – which is how he acquired his nickname!

Bandoola was exactly the same age as Bill and the two had quickly become firm friends. Bandoola was a huge elephant: standing nearly three metres tall. But he was clever, too, and had a mischievous sense of humour. Sometimes he would tease the workers by pretending that he couldn't push a log, before picking it up like a toy. A master elephant trainer called Po Toke had raised Bandoola with kindness and respect. He soon taught Bill how to train all elephants in his way.

Things changed after the Second World War broke out. In 1942 the Japanese army invaded Burma. Bill and his elephants joined a Special Forces Unit that helped build bridges and ferry supplies so the British army could fight back. But the Japanese continued to advance. Soon Bill found he needed to evacuate, with 53 elephants and 64 women and children in his care. The only way out was a long and dangerous march to India, through thick jungle and over rugged mountains. Bandoola led the way: he was now acting as the elephants' commanding officer.

After many exhausting days they reached the cliff. It looked too steep for elephants to climb. But Bill and his team didn't give up. Everyone worked to cut steps just big enough to make an elephant pathway. The work took several days, and at times they could hear distant enemy gunfire, but at last they were ready. The climb was painfully slow: it took each elephant three hours to reach the top, and if one had fallen, it would have knocked down all the others behind. But eventually, they made it. They would soon be in India – Bill and Bandoola had saved the day.

JUDY

THE PRISONERS' HEROIC DOG

Snap! Judy leaped up just as the crocodile's jaws slammed shut. The ferocious teeth grazed her shoulder but missed their grip. Before the crocodile could lunge again, a volley of shots rang out from the soldiers behind. The great reptile slipped back down into the murky waters of the swamp.

It was a narrow escape. The soldiers patched up the dog's wound. They had saved her life – but they were only repaying the favour. After all, this plucky pointer had done the same for them many times. And they knew they would need her help again if they were to survive the long jungle trek ahead.

Judy was born in Shanghai, China, in 1936. For a while she lived with a shopkeeper, who named her Shudi. One day some visiting sailors from the British warship HMS *Gnat* decided to buy her as a mascot. They changed her name to Judy, and she quickly proved very useful on the ship. One night her keen hearing alerted the crew to river pirates trying to sneak on board. She was also able to hear the high-pitched whine of incoming aircraft long before the crew could, and would keep barking until they had passed.

HER KEEN HEARING ALERTED THE CREW TO RIVER PIRATES

Soon some of the crew were transferred to another ship, HMS *Grasshopper*, and took Judy with them. When war was declared, this ship sailed to the British stronghold of Singapore to help protect it. On 8 February 1942, the Japanese army attacked, and for nine days a fierce battle raged. HMS *Grasshopper* fled to the islands of the Dutch East Indies (now Indonesia). As they sailed away, Judy heard the sound of an approaching Japanese aircraft. She barked her alarm but it was too late: the ship had been hit by several bombs. It started to sink.

The crew took to the lifeboats and managed to reach a nearby island, but they had lost Judy. Luckily, one sailor returned to the sinking ship in search of supplies and found her trapped behind some fallen lockers. The sailor brought her back to the island on a raft, together with all the supplies he could salvage.

The men were delighted to have Judy back. With her keen nose, she sniffed out a hidden spring under the beach, giving them vital fresh water. About a week later, the crew were able to make their way to the much bigger island of Sumatra, where they planned to meet up with British troops on the other side. Crossing the island meant a dangerous

five-week trek through dense jungle.

But Judy helped protect them. She looked out for enemy soldiers and once even spotted a tiger that was stalking them. In turn, they saved her from the crocodile.

Unfortunately, by the time the crew reached the port, the other British troops had left. The Japanese army soon arrived and immediately captured them. For the next three years the crew were prisoners of war. Life was very tough. They were forced to work hard in the tropical heat, and many suffered from diseases such as malaria. Judy stayed with them throughout, keeping their spirits up, protecting them from snakes and alerting them whenever guards were approaching. She was adopted by a new owner, Frank Williams, who looked after her and shared his rations with her. When the guards tried to take Judy away, Frank persuaded them to register her as a prisoner of war.

The prisoners were moved from camp to camp. Frank taught Judy to lie still inside a rice sack, so that he could take her with them without the guards knowing. Once, the boat in which they were travelling was hit by a torpedo and sunk. Many men

drowned but once again Judy survived. She even saved passengers by bringing them pieces of floating wood to cling on to. Frank couldn't believe it when she was reunited with him at the next camp. She bounded into his arms in delight.

Judy stayed with Frank until the War ended. 'She saved my life in so many ways,' he said. 'The greatest was giving me a reason to live.' During the very last week the Japanese guards decided to shoot Judy, blaming her for an outbreak of lice in the camp. But Frank sent her into the jungle to hide, and she didn't return until the

Japanese had left the camp.

After the War, Frank smuggled Judy back to Britain on a troop ship and in 1946 she was awarded the Dickin Medal. Word soon spread about her adventures and she became a celebrity – she even appeared on the radio, with her barks broadcast around the world! When she died in 1950, she was buried in a specially made RAF coat.

GI JOE

A TOP-SPEED PIGEON

On the morning of 18 October 1943, at an airbase in Italy, the US Army Air Force were preparing for action. Engines roared and propellers started to turn as bombers rumbled out onto the runway. Their mission was to bomb the German positions around the small village of Calvi Vecchia so that Allied troops could capture the town. The pilots strapped on their flying goggles. In just five minutes they would be taking off. They waited for the signal to fly.

Just then, a bird appeared from the sky. A pigeon! Flying at top speed, it zoomed across the airfield and straight for the pigeon loft, where it knew food would be waiting. Its handler recognized the bird immediately: this was GI Joe, one of his most handsome pigeons. He reached for the tube attached to GI Joe's leg. Pulling out a tiny scroll of paper, he read the message on it with shaking hands – then he rushed out onto the runway. 'Stop!' he shouted. 'Stop! Stop!'

GI Joe was a homing pigeon, specially bred to carry important messages where radio communication was impossible. The message he brought on this fateful morning came from the British troops in Calvi Vecchia, and it could not have been more important. It said that the British 169th Infantry Brigade had now advanced and captured the town. The Germans had retreated. There was no need for the bombing raid that the British troops had earlier requested.

Immediately, the bombing mission was halted. The aircraft returned to their hangars, where the pilots removed their goggles and stepped down from the cockpits. GI Joe was just in time! Had he arrived five minutes later, the planes would have taken off, and their bombs would have fallen on their own troops and on the villagers of Calvi Vecchia. The pigeon's message had saved around 1,000 lives – and, amazingly, he had sped across the 32 kilometres between the village and the airbase in only 20 minutes.

GI Joe had hatched in March 1943 at the US breeding station in Algiers, North Africa, so he was just seven months old when he completed his amazing mission in Italy. This brave bird was later awarded the Dickin Medal, the first non-British animal to receive one. He later retired to Detroit Zoo, USA, where he died in 1961 at the ripe old pigeon age of 18.

SHEILA

A SHEEPDOG WHO SAVED LIVES

Brrrr! Shepherd John Dagg closed the gate behind the sheep and blew on his hands. It was a cold, foggy December day in the Cheviot Hills, on the border between England and Scotland. He was looking forward to tramping the snow off his boots and getting home to his warm cottage. Sheila, his sheepdog, wagged her tail impatiently.

As John turned down the lane, however, the sound of aircraft engines low overhead stopped him in his tracks. He could see nothing through the fog but he knew something wasn't right.

Moments later, there was a huge bang. It could mean only one thing: the plane had crashed. Sheila's ears pricked up. 'Come on girl,' said John. 'We have to help. Quick!'

Together the man and his dog scrambled up the hillside, battling through deep snowdrifts. They were joined by Frank Moscrop, another shepherd, who had also heard the crash. Sheila bounded ahead, disappearing into the fog. The men followed the sound of her barking and soon found her at the top, staring down the other side.

It was difficult to see anything through the blizzard, but the men could just make out the shape of an aircraft lying on the hillside, its nose crumpled by the impact. They recognized it as a US air force Flying Fortress bomber. The plane must have got lost in the bad weather.

Had anybody survived the crash? There was only one way to find out. But instead of heading to the aircraft, Sheila led the men in another direction, towards the rocks. There, Sheila found four airmen, who had escaped from the wreck of their plane and were sheltering in a crevice. One was badly injured.

John gave the men first aid. Then, with Sheila's help, he led the party down the hillside. As they reached his cottage, the aircraft's bombs exploded with a huge boom, shattering

two windows. It was a close call, but thanks to Sheila, four men's lives had been saved.

Later they learned, sadly, that two of their companions had died in the crash – but three others had also found their way to safety.

John and Frank received the British Empire Medal for their bravery, and Sheila was awarded the Dickin Medal. She was the first non-military dog to receive this honour. After the War, Sheila had puppies and John sent one to America to the family of Sergeant Turner – one of the airmen who died.

BAMSE

A SEA-FARING DOG

Bamse the St Bernard grew up in the remote town of Honningsvåg in the very north of Norway. Bamse – which is pronounced *Bum-ser* – means 'teddy bear'. The Hafto family named him this because, although he was huge and powerful, he was also gentle and cuddly. When their daughter Vigdis fell ill, Bamse stayed by her bedside for 12 nights to look after her.

Erling Hafto, Vigdis's father, always took Bamse to sea with him. After the outbreak of the Second World War, his boat *Thorodd* joined the Royal Norwegian Navy as a patrol vessel. Bamse was soon made ship's mascot. In April 1940, when the German army invaded Norway, *Thorodd* escaped across the North Sea to Scotland. The boat was converted to a minesweeper.

The crew loved Bamse. During battles, he would ride at the front of the boat wearing a metal hat. Back in harbour, he helped look after them, rounding them up from the pub when it was time to return to the ship and, if fights broke out, putting his huge paws on their shoulders to calm them down. Once, he pushed a thief into the harbour to stop him attacking one of the crew. On another occasion he jumped into the sea to save a sailor who had fallen overboard, staying with him until both were rescued.

For all Norwegians living in Britain during the War, Bamse became a symbol of hope that they would one day return home. He was promoted to mascot for the entire Royal Norwegian Navy, and a photo of him wearing his sailor's cap was a popular Christmas card.

In his new home of Montrose he was also very popular. Everybody knew him. He wore a special bus pass on his collar, and – in his sailor's cap – would board the bus by himself and ride to nearby Dundee. At the local pub, people poured him beer in a bowl, and he often visited the baker, waiting patiently outside for leftovers.

Bamse died in Montrose in July 1944. At his funeral, hundreds of townsfolk lined the route and the crews of six Norwegian ships provided a guard of honour. In 2006 a bronze statue of Bamse was unveiled in Montrose. Vigdis Hafto herself came to see the ceremony – and three years later, school children from Montrose unveiled another statue of him in her home town of Honningsvåg. This big, special dog had helped make lifelong friendships between the people of Norway and Scotland.

BUS TICKET
Bamse
SCOTLAND BUS CO

LIN WANG

THE EVER-WORKING ELEPHANT

It is often said that elephants never forget. By the time Lin Wang passed away, at the grand old age of 86, he had lived in three countries and had more stories to tell than most people can ever dream of.

Lin Wang was a working Asian elephant. He had started life in the jungles of Burma where he used his great strength to carry logs through the jungle. At the age of 26 he was captured by Japanese forces who had entered Burma while fighting the Chinese during World War Two. His new masters made him carry military supplies and ammunition. Hauling these heavy loads through swollen rivers and slippery mountainsides was tough work. Many soldiers succumbed to exhaustion and tropical diseases, such as malaria. But Lin Wang kept going.

In 1943 the Chinese army recaptured Lin Wang and 12 other working elephants from the Japanese. For the animals, the work continued, whichever side they were on. And when the War ended, life didn't get any easier. The elephant team marched out of Burma and into China, as far as the city of Guangzhou. This exhausting journey lasted a year and a half. Along the way, the soldiers trained the elephants to do some simple tricks, such as walking backwards, turning around, and crouching down and standing up again.

After the War ended, Lin Wang was sent by boat to the island of Taiwan, along with two female elephants. Sadly, one of his companions died soon after the voyage and the other died four years later, after working hard alongside Lin Wang building railways. Now Lin Wang found himself alone.

Finally, in 1952, Lin Wang retired. He was transferred to the Yuanshan Zoo in Taipei, Taiwan's capital, where he joined four-year-old Ma Lan, a young female elephant. At last he could enjoy a well-deserved rest. Occasionally he performed some of his tricks but mostly he just enjoyed the company of his new friend. Lin Wang became famous throughout Taiwan, and in 1986 he and Ma Lan moved to a new zoo. In 1997, to celebrate his 80th birthday, a special tropical forest enclosure was built for them. It was just like the wet, steamy jungles where Lin Wang had grown up, only this time he didn't have to work.

When Lin Wang passed away, in February 2003, he was believed to be the oldest elephant in captivity. The Taiwanese people mourned him in the traditional way, lighting incense sticks and burning paper money. Today his name lives on in a special conservation programme that helps protect elephants across south-east Asia.

ANTIS

THE PILOT'S BEST FRIEND

The roar of the stricken aircraft still rang in the ears of Václav Bozděch as he crept towards the dark farmhouse. Terrified he might be discovered, he eased open the door. There was nobody there – thank goodness. He crept back to his injured companion, Pierre Duval, helping him inside before slumping to the floor beside him.

Safe at last. Or were they? Suddenly, the two men heard a scratching sound from behind them. 'Who goes there?' shouted Václav, drawing his revolver. 'Come out, or I'll shoot!'

A skinny German shepherd puppy emerged, wagging his tail feebly. The men breathed a sigh of relief. Václav dug out a frozen bar of chocolate. Using an old frying pan, he managed to melt some and feed it to the starving puppy. Soon that little tail was wagging harder.

The year was 1940, early in the Second World War. Václav and Pierre had been flying aircraft over the German front from Saint Dizier airbase in north-east France. Václav was Czech and Pierre, the pilot, was French. Hit by anti-aircraft fire, they had crash-landed in no man's land. Now they had to reach safety before they were captured.

Before dawn, they left the farmhouse, shutting the puppy inside with the last of their chocolate and a frying pan of water. But as they walked away, they could hear his pitiful howling. He was going to give them away. With a heavy heart, Václav returned to the house. But when he saw the puppy, he knew there was only one thing he could do – he picked him up, tucking him snugly into his flying jacket. He had just made a friend for life.

Luckily, the French troops found the two men before the Germans did. Soon they were back at their base, where a doctor tended to Pierre while Václav was reunited with the other airmen. Over the following weeks, the puppy grew stronger and took to sleeping at the foot of Václav's bed. He quickly became a firm favourite with the airmen, who named him Antis, after their favourite Czech aircraft. On 10 March a German air raid forced the squadron to move to a new base; Antis had heard the approaching bombers before anybody else could, growling when they approached.

Soon Václav and Pierre started flying missions again – and now Antis came with them. He curled up quietly at Václav's feet, not worried when the firing started. In June, however, France surrendered to Germany and the airmen knew they had to get out. Their plan was to return to Britain and regroup. They headed for the station, but on the platform they found a huge crowd all struggling to board the train. Antis ran down to a cattle wagon at the far end. The men followed, and inside they found a woman sharing some chocolate with her two daughters. Antis must

have smelt it! One girl offered him a piece – and this time, it didn't need melting. Antis and Václav clambered inside to join the family on their long journey.

From Montpellier, in the south of France, the airmen sailed to the British base of Gibraltar, in Spain. Here they boarded the NV *Northmoor*, a ship bound for England. Animals weren't allowed on board but Václav would not leave Antis behind. Once on deck, he climbed down a ladder on the outside and whistled for Antis to join him. The dog plunged into the harbour and swam 100m to the ship! Václav wrapped him up in his greatcoat and smuggled him aboard.

During the voyage, Antis stayed hidden below decks – until the *Northmoor* developed engine problems and the passengers were transferred to another ship. At this point, a sailor spotted Antis's head popping out of Václav's kit bag. Luckily, he liked dogs so he said nothing. When they reached Liverpool, the crew's luggage was unloaded by crane. Only Václav knew that Antis was hiding inside one of the bags.

Václav joined RAF 311 Squadron, a Czech squadron based near Liverpool. Antis became their mascot. Just as in France, he was able to sense approaching bombers and would help give the alarm before an air raid. During one such raid on the nearby docks, he helped search for survivors. He managed to find a one-year-old child, even though his paws were injured by the burning rubble.

After a while, 311 Squadron moved south to Norfolk. Now Václav started flying missions again. Antis always watched his master take off and waited patiently for his safe return. When Václav's plane was hit one night, Antis seemed to know, and started

howling. Luckily, Václav got home safely. Soon Antis started flying with Václav again. Together, the pair completed 30 missions.

Antis and Václav both survived the War and afterwards returned to Czechoslovakia (now the Czech Republic). Unfortunately, they were no longer safe in Václav's homeland: the new communist government did not welcome anybody who had fought with the Allies during the War. In 1948, the two made one last daring escape together. Antis helped them avoid the sentry's searchlights and machine guns as they slipped over the border into West Germany – to safety.

Václav finally settled in England, where he became a British national. In 1949, Antis received the Dickin Medal for animal bravery. He passed away two years later, at the age of 14. Václav continued flying for the RAF, but he never got another dog: he knew none could ever measure up to Antis.

TACOMA

THE FIND-AND-SEEK DOLPHIN

It was dark on the ocean bed, too dark to see, but Tacoma the bottlenose dolphin had found what he was looking for. With one wiggle of his tail, he swam up towards the small boat above him. He took just seconds to reach the surface. With his long nose, he poked a plastic ball fixed on the front of the boat. Then he popped up his head, puffed through his blowhole and opened his mouth in a toothy grin.

Tacoma's trainers were waiting in the boat. They were thrilled to see him – and very excited that he had pressed the ball. This was a signal they had taught him: it meant that he might have found a dangerous mine on the seabed. The mine had been planted by the enemy, ready to explode when a large ship passed close by.

HE HAD FOUND A DANGEROUS MINE ON THE SEABED

The trainers tossed Tacoma a juicy fish as a reward. Then they gave him a special float to take down and mark the mine's position. Immediately, the dolphin flipped up his tail and disappeared beneath the surface to finish his work. Soon the navy divers would be able to locate the deadly mine and remove it safely.

In 2003 Tacoma was one of a team of nine specially trained dolphins used by the American and British navies during the Gulf War. The dolphins' job was to search for mines and other explosive devices that had been hidden underwater. Altogether they found more than 100 devices! Thanks to the dolphins, the ships were now able to deliver vital supplies to the soldiers.

Dolphins have been trained for use in warfare since the 1960s. They can dive much deeper than any human divers, and they can also find underwater objects using a special technique called echolocation (making clicking noises that bounce off an object and reveal its location). This helps them to find small things – such as mines – that no machine can detect. They can even find objects buried under 50 centimetres of mud!

But that's not all. As well as finding mines, dolphins can also patrol ports to look out for enemy divers, retrieve lost equipment, carry things down to divers working on the sea bed and lead lost divers back to their ship. These incredible animals will continue with their clever work – just so long as they get plenty of juicy fish in return!

SEA LION

A SWIMMING SENTRY

A trail of bubbles rose to the surface as the diver moved through the dark water, kicking steadily with his flippers. The explosive mine he was carrying could blow up a ship. Soon he would plant this deadly weapon on the sea bed and then swim silently away. Nobody would even know he'd been there.

Suddenly the diver felt something strike him from behind. He reached down to find a clamp on his leg. What was going on? He struggled to free himself, but it was no good. Next, a big animal zoomed past then popped up to stare at him, showing its dark eyes and whiskery muzzle. It was a sea lion – and he could swear it was grinning.

Luckily, the mine this diver was carrying wasn't real. In fact, he was a trainer, working at the US navy training centre in San Diego to train sea lions. And this sea lion had done its job perfectly. Once it had attached the clamp, a team waiting in the boat above could pull on the line and reel in the diver – just like a fish. The sea lion was now ready to clamp any

diver who might really want to attack a harbour or boat.

Sea lions are perfect for this kind of work. They are slick swimmers that can dive very deep, and do it over and over again. They also have sensitive underwater eyesight and hearing, allowing them to find objects in dark conditions. And they are very intelligent, so can learn new tasks and follow commands quickly. They can also hop on to land so they can pursue somebody out of the water, if necessary, and alert everyone in the vicinity with their loud honking.

As well as finding enemy divers, sea lions are trained to detect mines, find lost equipment and rescue survivors from plane crashes.

And, once trained, they can be prepared and sent within three days by ship, aircraft or land vehicle to do their work anywhere in the world. In 2003 they worked in a real-life conflict for the first time, helping protect British and American warships during the Gulf War.

Of course, the sea lions do not volunteer for this dangerous work – and some people think that it is unfair to use them. But at least these trained animals are not kept in a small tank. They spend most of their lives swimming happily in the sea, and only return to their trainers when they are needed.

ALEPPO ZOO

THE ANIMALS OF HOPE

It was hot. Very hot. Summer temperatures soar to over 45 degrees in the Syrian desert. Amir Khalil wiped the sweat from his brow. He knew the animals in the truck would be feeling the heat – and he watched the team splash water over their cages to keep them cool. Right now, though, he was more worried about the border guards. They were still arguing about the paperwork. Would they allow the truck through?

The date was 21 July 2017. For six years, a terrible civil war had been raging in Syria between the government and other groups who wanted to take control. The Syrian city of Aleppo had seen some of the worst fighting: many areas were reduced to rubble and food was running out for the people who still lived there.

It was not only the people who were suffering. Just outside Aleppo was a zoo called Magic World. Once there had been more than 300 animals there, but since the war started many had died. There was no food, no water, no medicine, and nobody left to care for them properly.

THERE WAS NO FOOD, NO WATER, NO MEDICINE

By the time Amir came to hear about the plight of Magic World, just 13 animals remained: five lions, two tigers, two spotted hyenas, two Asiatic black bears and two husky dogs. All were sick or starving. Amir was a veterinary surgeon from Egypt and he worked for an international organization called Four Paws that helped rescue animals during wartime. He knew he had to get the animals out of Syria – but he knew it wouldn't be easy.

The rescue mission took very careful planning: Amir and his team had to get special permission from officials on all sides. The plan was to drive the animals from Magic World to the border with Turkey, 150 kilometres away. This was the quickest route, but also very dangerous. There might be landmines along the rough, rubble-strewn road, and they also risked attack from bombers or snipers. They might even be targeted by kidnappers.

Eventually, the team were granted permission. During the night, the animals were loaded in their cages onto a truck and the convoy set off at first light. It was Friday, the Muslim holy day, when things were quieter: the team hoped that this might make their journey easier. Meanwhile, another convoy, without any animals, set off in another direction to fool anybody who might want to chase or stop them. In the real convoy, the animals in their cages stayed quiet, so they were able to drive out of the city without attracting too much attention.

When the convoy reached the border, the guards at first refused to let them through. But the team persisted. They explained that they had nothing to do with the war – they just wanted to help the animals. Eventually the guards opened the border. They gave the team only one hour to transfer the cages onto a vehicle waiting on the other side. Soldiers and guards put down their rifles to help with the hard work. Fierce fighters smiled and embraced, taking selfies with the animals.

HIS HEART STOPPED BEATING WITH THE STRESS OF THE JOURNEY

Once the team had reached Turkey, they drove through the night. The animals were weak and urgently needed to get to the animal rescue centre in Karacabey, where a team of experts were waiting. Most of the animals were in a bad way: one hyena was nearly blind and the bears had broken teeth from chewing the bars of their cage. Sultan the tiger almost died: his heart stopped beating from the stress of the journey, but luckily a vet was able to revive him.

The animals waited three weeks at the rescue centre as the team made arrangements for their new life. With special care from experts, they were slowly getting better and stronger. On 28 July, a second mission brought the two lions and two huskies that they had not been able to fit on the truck first time round. Now all 13 animals had been rescued.

On 10 August, the animals were flown from Turkey to Al-Ma'wa, their new home in Jordan. At this special sanctuary, they no longer had to worry about noise and bombs. They had large enclosures in peace and quiet among the olive groves, where they could begin to recover. The tigers relaxed and cooled off in their pools. The bears eagerly gobbled up the food provided for them.

Amir is very proud of the team's rescue mission. He has seen how animals have brought people together in a time of war: 'We should never give up,' he says. 'Animals can light a little candle of hope in all this darkness.'

RECKLESS

THE LUCKY, HUNGRY HORSE

'Go on, help yourself!' said the soldier, as he held out a peanut-butter sandwich. Reckless gobbled it down greedily. This horse would consume anything: eggs, mashed potato, Coca-Cola. Once she even ate a hat! The soldiers didn't mind, they were happy to share their rations. In fact, they let her go anywhere – even inside their tents. She was a hero.

It was 1953, at the height of the Korean War. British and American troops were locked in heavy fighting and many soldiers had died. Reckless was a pack horse and she worked for the US Marine Corps, carrying ammunition to the men on the front line and rescuing the wounded. The conditions were very tough, with freezing winter weather, but she never stopped working.

Reckless got her name because of her dangerous work. But she had not always worked for the army: she had once been a racehorse. Her young Korean owner had sold her to the marines for US$250. He had loved his horse, but his sister had been injured by a landmine, and he needed money to pay for her operation.

The marines trained Reckless as an ammunition carrier and they soon discovered she was a very fast learner. She knew how to step over barbed wire and how to gallop to a bunker when shells started falling. She also knew how to find her way unaccompanied, which meant she could make many trips on her own.

In late March 1953, Reckless found herself at the battle of Outpost Vegas, one of the fiercest battles of the War. On one single day she made 51 trips to and from the front. Shells exploded around her and bullets whizzed past. She was wounded twice, but she kept going: she walked more than 56 kilometres and carried more than five tonnes of ammunition. She helped save many soldiers' lives.

The Korean War ended in July that same year and Reckless was shipped back to America as a hero. She arrived in San Francisco on 10 November 1954, which was the birthday of the US Marine Corps. At the birthday ball she received a hero's welcome – and decided to eat both the cake and the flowers!

Reckless died in 1968 at the Marine Corps base in California. She received many awards, including the Dickin Medal for animal bravery. But perhaps her finest moment came on 15 June 1957, when the proud marines promoted her to the special position of Staff Sergeant Reckless.

LUCCA

THE DOG OF 400 MISSIONS

'Help!' shouted Corporal Juan Rodriguez. 'Lucca's been hit.' With the explosion still ringing in his ears, he crouched down beside the dog. He could see that she was badly injured, but she was still breathing. He cradled her head in his lap as he tied a tourniquet around her leg to stop the bleeding. 'Come on girl,' he whispered. 'You can make it.'

Lucca was a search dog for the US Marine Corps, and served for six years during the wars in Iraq and Afghanistan. A handsome cross between a German shepherd and a Belgian Malinois, she was trained in Israel and the USA. Much of her special training took place in hot dry places, such as Arizona, to prepare her for the deserts where she would be working.

Few dogs were as clever as Lucca, or as brave. On patrol with the marines, she would walk out in front, off the leash. She searched roads, buildings and vehicles, using her sensitive nose to sniff out ammunition and explosives. She detected dangerous objects 40 times, and her work probably saved hundreds of soldier's lives. During the 400 missions she completed, not one soldier died.

FEW DOGS WERE AS CLEVER AS LUCCA, OR AS BRAVE

It was on Lucca's last mission, on 23 March 2012 that her luck ran out. She was on patrol in Afghanistan – searching ahead of her platoon, as usual. She had already detected one IED (Improvised Explosive Device) buried in the ground. Unfortunately, she hadn't noticed another one nearby. It detonated right underneath her.

Amazingly, Lucca survived the explosion. Thanks to the quick actions of Juan Rodriguez and his team – who gave her all the care they would give to another marine – her wound was patched up, and within ten minutes a helicopter had arrived to airlift her to a military hospital. The vets had to amputate her injured front left leg, but just 10 days later she had made a full recovery and was walking again. Her eyesight and hearing recovered completely.

That year, Lucca retired. She was flown back to California, USA, where she went to live in peace with Gunnery Sergeant Chris Willingham, who had first trained her. 'Lucca is the only reason I made it home to my family,' says Chris, who had also served with her in Afghanistan. When Lucca won the Dickin Medal, on 5 April 2016, she became a TV celebrity across the USA.

MOUNTAIN MULES

BRINGING HELP AND HOPE

Cheers rang out as the mules appeared. Help had arrived – at last! The animals patiently picked their way over the rubble and past the ruined buildings. The villagers rushed forward to help the soldiers unload the heavy saddle bags. Some contained tents and blankets. Others had sacks of food, such as wheat, flour and high-energy biscuits. Anxious hands awaited to distribute the supplies to those most in need.

It was October 2005, one week after a devastating earthquake had struck the mountainous region of Kashmir in northern Pakistan. Thousands of people had died and even more were left homeless. With winter on the way, people urgently needed food and shelter. The army was trying its best to help, but with the roads blocked and cut off by landslides, their vehicles could not get through. A special force of 1,000 soldiers were still stuck in the city of Rawalpindi, unable to reach the disaster zone.

THESE TOUGH, HARDY ANIMALS COULD COVER THE ROUGHEST AND STEEPEST TERRAIN

Thankfully, mules came to the rescue. They might seem like unlikely heroes, but these tough, hardy animals could cover the roughest and steepest terrain to places that no vehicle or machine could reach. Each could carry a load of up to 72kg – the weight of a man – and cover 26 kilometres without resting. What's more, mules could keep going high in the mountains, where the air was so thin that people quickly became exhausted.

Some people in Pakistan used to laugh at mules and their trainers. They had never understood why the army wanted them. Mules were not as big as horses or camels, they said, so why waste time on all that special training? They wondered why mules were given special high-energy foods, such as chickpeas and sugar, and had dedicated vets to look after them.

But the mule handlers knew better. During wartime, when supplies needed carrying, mules were the most reliable pack animals. They would keep going by themselves, even when gunfire or shelling forced their handlers to turn back. Now, in peace time, the mules were proving that they were just as important. Many mules had been killed in the earthquake, but the army brought in more from elsewhere. Together, these brave animals carried hundreds of tonnes of supplies to the stricken villages and ferried the wounded to field hospitals. Nobody laughed at mules any more – these animals were heroes!

ROSELLE

A GUIDE DOG HERO

Down, down, down. Step after step after step. Michael Hingson and his guide dog Roselle pressed on together into the smoke-filled darkness. The people around them were scared. They could smell the flames and the suffocating fumes of jet fuel. But Michael and Roselle stayed calm. They walked steadily, one step at a time. On they went. Down, down, down . . .

THEY COULD SMELL THE FLAMES

The date was 11 September 2001 – now known around the world as 9/11. An aircraft hijacked by terrorists had just crashed into the North Tower of the World Trade Center, one of two main towers that made up this huge 110-storey building in New York City. Known as 'the twin towers', these soaring skyscrapers dominated the city skyline. Michael Hingson worked on the 78th floor. He was blind, so he always brought his guide dog, Roselle, with him to the office. A labrador retriever with a gentle face and a beautiful pale coat, she was very popular among his colleagues.

Today, Michael had come in early for a meeting. Roselle was sleeping under his desk, when, at 8.46 a.m. the aircraft struck the building 15 floors above them. The impact woke her immediately and she sat straight up, ready to work. Everybody in the office had heard the noise and felt the tower shudder. At first, they didn't understand what had happened: they looked out at the clear blue sky and could see nothing wrong. Then smoke began to billow past the windows and suddenly they felt the whole building lurch sideways. They knew they had to get out. Fast.

Roselle knew exactly what to do. 'Forward' said Michael, grasping her harness. This is one of the first commands a guide dog learns and Roselle was well-trained. Burning debris was now falling past the windows and it was too dangerous to use the lifts. Roselle guided Michael to Stairway B, at the centre of the building.

From the 78th floor, it was a very long way down: 1,463 steps. The stairway rang with the noise of frightened people. But Michael and Roselle didn't panic. They had been together for about two years and made the perfect team. Roselle listened out for Michael's voice. Michael could tell from the rhythm of her breathing and the tension on her harness when she was ready for his next command. Roselle waited for Michael at the top of each new flight of stairs, so he knew they were about to descend again, then Michael would urge her forward.

Soon, around 30 people were following the

pair as they continued down, step by step. The further they descended, the more tired they became, and Michael could tell that Roselle was finding it hard to keep going. But they dared not stop: the building might collapse at any moment. Automatic sprinklers activated by the smoke made the floors wet, and Michael was worried that Roselle might slip. About halfway down they met the firemen who were heading up to the floors above. Roselle greeted them affectionately and they patted her head.

Everybody found some comfort in that friendly wagging tail.

Finally, after about an hour, Michael and his colleagues reached the ground floor. But still they weren't safe. Roselle led them out into the street, which was filled with the noise of people running and the wail of the emergency sirens. As they turned away from the burning building, the South Tower – which had been hit by another hijacked aircraft – collapsed. A colossal cloud of sand and rubble rose up into the air, choking them

with dust and making it difficult to breathe. But Roselle continued to guide Michael, not stopping once until they reached the safety of a subway station.

The subway train took them safely back to Michael's home. Once there, Roselle was at last able to relax. She was soon playing in the garden with Linnie, an older guide dog of Michael's, as if it were any normal day. Michael turned on the news to find out what had happened. He learned that at 10.28 a.m. – just 30 minutes after the South Tower came down – the North Tower had also collapsed. They had got out just in time.

Nearly 3,000 people died that day. And had it not been for Roselle, Michael and his colleagues might have been among them.

On 5 March 2002 Roselle received the Dickin Medal for animal bravery. She shared it with Salty, another guide dog who had also rescued his owner, Omar Rivera, from the North Tower that day. It was only the second time the Dickin Medal had been awarded to two animals jointly. In March 2007 Roselle retired from guiding. When she died, in June 2011, she was voted American Hero Dog of the Year by nearly half a million people.

GIANT AFRICAN RATS

THE RODENTS WHO RESCUE

Sniff, sniff, sniff. Scratch, scratch, scratch. A twitchy, whiskery nose pokes and probes the dusty ground. Sharp little claws scrabble away at the soil. It's a rat. And it has important and dangerous work to do. There's no time to waste!

Surprised? You might think that rats make unlikely heroes. But this Gambian pouched rat is different from an ordinary rat. For a start, it's as big as a small cat. What's more, it's wearing a harness around its shoulders, with a long lead attached, held by the rat's trainer.

Not only is this rat big; it is also very clever. Working with its trainer, it is searching for landmines. Here in the southern African country of Mozambique, many of these terrible weapons are left over from the long civil war that ended in 1992. They are buried just under the ground, waiting to explode if anybody treads on them. Today, even years after the war ended, hidden mines still kill or injure many people.

The rat's trainers have taught it to use its super-sensitive nose to recognize the smell

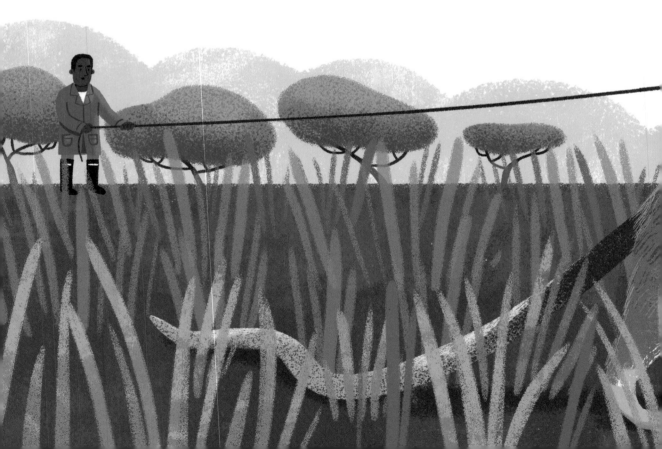

of explosives. Because its body is much lighter than a person's, it can walk over a mine without causing it to explode. Once the rat sniffs out a mine, it scratches the ground for a few seconds. When the trainer sees this, he makes a clicking noise and the rat will stop digging and come over to nibble a banana – its reward. The bomb disposal experts now know where the mine is, so they can defuse it.

This amazing project is run by an organization from Belgium called APOPO. Experts discovered that these rats are much better at finding mines than humans using metal detectors. Metal detectors find any old metal under the ground, but rats start digging only when they detect explosives. In just 20 minutes, a rat can clear an area of 200 square metres that would take humans up to three days to search!

In Mozambique the rats have already located thousands of landmines. They have done their job so well that they are now also helping clear mines in other parts of the world, such as Cambodia. But it's not all work for the clever rodents. Their trainers make sure they get plenty of playtime back in their cages. Some people don't like rats – but here in Mozambique people love and admire them. After all, these rats are saving lives.

ARAMIS

THE EAGLE DRONE-DESTROYER

Whoosh! Aramis the eagle folds back his wings and dives. Ahead of him, something white hovers in the air like a tiny helicopter. A drone. Its propellers whine like mosquitoes as it tries to gain height and escape. But it's too late – the great bird is too fast. He spreads his huge wings wide, stretches out his sharp talons and plucks the machine from the sky. Bang! The annoying buzzing comes to an abrupt stop.

Aramis is one of four golden eagles being trained in France to help capture and destroy electronic drones. Today, many people use drones to take pictures and have fun. But the army are worried that these machines could be dangerous if they fall into the wrong hands: terrorists might use them to carry weapons, drop bombs, or crash them into flying aircraft.

It is possible to shoot drones down, or to stop them from flying by jamming their electronic signals. But these methods can be difficult and expensive – and scientists now think that eagles might be able to do the job better.

These big, fierce birds of prey are perfectly equipped for catching drones. In the wild, their amazing eyesight allows them to spot a rabbit from three kilometres away. They are also very fast and agile, able to twist and turn in the sky to catch a flying bird. Compared to hunting their natural prey, hunting a drone is easy.

What's more, an eagle doesn't just smash a drone into bits, like a bullet would. This might cause dangerous pieces to fall on people underneath. Instead, it carries it away somewhere safe. Eagles are strong enough to carry prey weighing up to 3kg, which is much heavier than a small drone. Once they land, their handler offers them a piece of meat, so they put the drone down and it can be taken away.

Aramis and his eagle companions have been used to drones ever since they hatched from the egg. As little chicks, they were raised on top of one. Now they are growing up and learning to catch drones. The scientists and trainers still have more

AS LITTLE CHICKS, THEY WERE RAISED ON TOP OF A DRONE

work to do. They need to make sure that the drones don't harm the eagles – and that the eagles always obey instructions. But one day soon, these birds may be doing a very important job in protecting us from danger.

ANIMALS IN WARFARE

People have used animals in warfare since ancient times. An illustration made in around 2,500 BC shows horses pulling chariots in the kingdom of Sumeria (near present-day Iraq). By 1,100 BC the Hindu dynasties of India were fighting with elephants. Since then, countless animals have played lots of different roles in wars all over the world. And many have lost their lives.

A HEAVY LOAD

For thousands of years, strong animals such as horses and donkeys have worked as beasts of burden: pulling carts, carrying supplies and transporting wounded soldiers. Certain animals are suited to particular environments – mules can carry supplies over mountains, elephants can crash a path through jungles and camels can trek through deserts without needing much water.

An amazing number of animals have served humans in this way. By 1918, the last year of the First World War, the British forces had 828,000 horses, mules, camels, donkeys and oxen. To feed all the British horses and mules throughout the whole war, it took nearly six million tonnes of oats and hay. Sadly, many war horses didn't survive: in June 1941 the German army gathered 625,000 horses for the invasion of Russia – and 180,000 died during the first six months.

INTO BATTLE

Once, all armies used soldiers mounted on horseback – known as cavalry. Famous leaders such as Alexander the Great would ride into battle on their favourite horse. During the First World War (1914–1918), modern vehicles and long-range weapons meant that horses became less important and by the Second World War (1939–1945), they were seldom used in fighting. Today, the Indian army has the only regular cavalry unit in the world.

Some ancient empires, including the Romans and Carthaginians, attacked their enemies with elephants. But this didn't always work: Roman poet Pliny the Elder wrote about enemy armies who drove squealing pigs towards the elephants, which frightened the huge beasts and caused them to charge back into their own lines.

Dogs have also been sent into battle. The Romans trained Molossian dogs, a now-extinct breed, to attack their enemies, even kitting them out in spiky armour. During the 1500s, the Spanish Conquistadors used Alaunt dogs, also now extinct, to attack the native armies of Central America. By the First and Second World Wars, dogs were mostly used for search-and-rescue operations or as guard dogs.

OTHER ANIMAL WORK

Animals have had many other wartime jobs. Dogs have often carried messages, and for centuries homing pigeons have provided communication when no other means were available. In 1907, a German pharmacist called Julius Neubronner was the first to use birds for aerial photography, when he fixed a small camera to a pigeon's body.

Dogs also hunted down the rats that swarmed through the trenches in the First World War, while cats have searched for rodents on warships. Dogs' highly sensitive noses mean they can seek out hidden things, from explosives to injured soldiers. Other animals whose detection skills have proved useful include rats, dolphins and even canaries, which can detect the smell of poison gas.

TRAINING

Intelligent animals such as dogs can learn new skills, and during the Second World War, the US army set up a unit called the K9 Corps, which trained dogs for war. Around 10,000 dogs went through a ten-week training course, where they learned to ride on military vehicles, cope with the noise of gunfire and even wear gas masks. After the war it took another two years to retrain them as pets.

Today special training schools teach dogs skills such as mine detection, while at the US Navy Marine Mammal Program in San Diego, California, dolphins and sea lions are trained to search for and retrieve objects underwater.

RAISING THE SPIRITS

Even when not working, animals play a vital role during wartime. Many – including dogs, cats, goats, bears, eagles and even monkeys – have acted as regimental mascots, bringing soldiers a feeling of pride. And, perhaps most important of all, animals bring companionship. For soldiers who may be hurt, frightened and far from home, the affection and devotion of an animal can help raise the spirits, and help them get through the hard times until the war comes to an end.

WHY ARE ANIMALS BRAVE?

This book is full of amazing stories about animal bravery. Dogs, horses, pigeons, elephants, dolphins and many, many more have all risked their lives to help the people who look after them. Many of these animals have been injured, or have even died. It's no wonder we call them heroes. But why do animals perform these heroic actions? If we look closer, we can see that much of their behaviour comes from their natural instincts.

ONE OF THE GANG

Dogs are amazingly loyal animals. Many of the canine heroes in this book stayed with their human masters even when bullets were flying or their ship was sinking. You're probably wondering why they didn't just run away. But this loyalty makes more sense when we remember that dogs are descended from wolves, which are pack animals. In the wild, a wolf pack works together as a team to look after each other. Each member has a different position in the pack. The 'alpha wolf' is in charge. The others respect it: they know that by following their leader, the pack will stick together and each individual will find it easier to survive.

A well-trained dog sees its master as an alpha wolf. Its instinct tells it to be obedient and do what it is told because its master will provide food, shelter and protection. This instinct is so strong that some dogs will risk their own life to protect their master and his companions.

Horses in the wild also live in groups with a ranking system. Usually the alpha horse walks in front and the others follow behind, in order of importance. A well-trained horse sees its rider or trainer as an alpha horse. It will overcome its instinct to flee from danger and instead follow its instinct to stay with its leader, who it trusts to protect it. This means that a rider can train a horse to stand still, even with the noise of exploding bombs all around.

EDIBLE REWARDS

Food is the best reward for animals (and sometimes humans!). Animals can be trained to do difficult or dangerous things because they know they will receive a tasty reward in return.

Of course, animals are also very good at finding food by themselves, and some have super-sensory powers and can find things in places where we can't. A dog uses its amazing sense of smell to help it find food. This means that it can also be trained to sniff out difficult-to-find things during wartime, such as explosives buried underground. Its reward comes in knowing it has pleased its master, who will then continue to feed and look after it.

Dolphins have a very special sense called echolocation. They make a stream of high-pitched clicking noises that bounce off objects underwater. The echoes reveal exactly where the objects are, so the dolphins can avoid them or – if it's a school of fish – catch them. People have trained dolphins to use this skill to locate underwater explosives and enemy divers. For their hard work, the dolphins' reward is (you guessed it!) fish.

FINDING THEIR WAY

Many animals are brilliant at finding their way, without using maps or sat nav! Birds are especially good at this. Many migrate huge distances every year, and navigate right back to their nest site, often crossing mountains, deserts and oceans along the way.

Homing pigeons have an especially strong instinct to find their way home. People have made the most of this, using the birds to carry important messages when radios and other means of communication are not possible. They know that when they release a pigeon with a tiny message fixed to its leg, it will fly straight back to its home at the army base. Pigeons can fly at 140 kph, and can carry a message for 1,000 kilometres in less than 12 hours!

Birds find their way using a combination of skills. They use UV-sensitive eyesight to follow hidden light on the horizon, can memorize landmarks such as rivers, and can even find their direction from stars in the night sky. Scientists have also discovered that pigeons have tiny particles of an element called magnetite in their brain, which allows them to work out where north is, just like using a compass.

INSPIRED BY ANIMALS

It's hard to judge whether or not animals can truly be called 'brave'. We often credit animals with human qualities, such as love, kindness and bravery, but animals do not always act for the same reasons. We do know, however, that animals do many things that – in human beings – would be considered acts of great courage. In times of war and danger, they earn our admiration, trust and gratitude. And often they inspire *us* to be brave, too.

HALL OF FAME

Many animal heroes have been awarded medals for their brave deeds, including the Dickin Medal. This special award was created in 1943 by Maria Dickin, who started the People's Dispensary for Sick Animals (PDSA). The award is for animals that have have shown great courage or devotion to their jobs. As of January 2019, it has been awarded 70 times, to many brave pigeons, dogs, horses, and one cat. Here are some photos of the real-life animal heroes in this book, alongside some of their human admirers!

WARRIOR, PAGE 16

TIRPITZ, PAGE 28

ROB, PAGE 30

CHIPS, PAGE 34

SIMON, PAGE 38

WOJTEK, PAGE 40

JET, PAGE 44

WINKIE, PAGE 46

WINKIE, PAGE 46

GI JOE, PAGE 54

LIN WANG, PAGE 60

ANTIS, PAGE 62

K-DOG, A TRAINED DOLPHIN
LIKE TACOMA, PAGE 66

SGT RECKLESS, PAGE 74

ROSELLE, PAGE 80

GLOSSARY

 AMBASSADOR
An official representative of a country or organization who tries to portray it in a positive way.

ANZAC
Slang word for a member of the Australian or New Zealand armed forces. The word stands for Australia and New Zealand Army Corps and was first used in the First World War.

ARMISTICE
A formal agreement made between two countries at war, to stop fighting.

D DECOY
Something or somebody used to mislead or confuse others – for example, by luring them into a trap or by leading them somewhere they can't cause harm.

DETONATE
To explode, or cause something to explode.

DEMOBILIZED
When soldiers and other military personnel are released from service with the armed forces, usually at the end of a war.

DITCH
To land an aircraft in the sea in an emergency. If an aircraft ditches successfully, its crew and passengers can usually get out and use their life rafts.

H HOWDAH
A large seat, usually with a canopy, that carries riders on the back of an elephant.

I IED
A home-made bomb, usually used by rebel forces who are not part of an army. It stands for Improvised Explosive Device.

L LANDMINE
A bomb that is placed in or under the ground, and explodes when somebody steps on it or a vehicle drives over it.

M
MAHOUT
A person who trains, rides and looks after a working elephant.

MENAGERIE
A captive collection of wild animals, either kept in private or on show to the public.

MINE
A type of bomb hidden in the ground or floating in the sea that explodes when a person, vehicle or ship passes over it.

MINESWEEPER
A military ship that searches for mines in the sea and destroys or removes them.

O
OBITUARY
An article (usually in a newspaper) published after somebody has died that tells the story of their life.

P
POSTHUMOUS
Describes things that happen after someone's death. A posthumous medal is one that is awarded after its recipient has died.

S
SABOTAGE
To damage or destroy something, such as a building or equipment, to prevent somebody else (such as an enemy army) from using it.

SHRAPNEL
Small pieces of metal that fly through the air when a bomb or similar weapon explodes. Shrapnel can kill and injure people.

T
TORPEDO
A long thin bomb, fired by a ship or aircraft, that travels underwater in order to destroy a ship or other target in the sea.

TOURNIQUET
A strip of cloth that is tied tightly around an arm or leg in order to stop it bleeding.

W
WESTERN FRONT
The main area of Europe in which most of the First World War fighting took place (mostly in Luxembourg, Belgium and France).

PUFFIN BOOKS

UK | USA | Canada | Ireland | Australia
India | New Zealand | South Africa

Puffin Books is part of the Penguin Random House group of companies
whose addresses can be found at global.penguinrandomhouse.com.

www.penguin.co.uk   www.puffin.co.uk   www.ladybird.co.uk

  Penguin
Random House
UK

First published 2019

001

Introduction copyright © Michael Morpurgo, 2019
Text copyright © Mike Unwin, 2019
Illustrations copyright © Rebecca Green, Richard Jones, Essi Kimpimäki, Hannah Peck, Miranda Sofroniou, 2019
The moral rights of the authors and illustrators have been asserted

Printed in Malaysia

A CIP catalogue record for this book is available from the British Library

ISBN: 978–0–241–37708–6

All correspondence to:
Puffin Books
Penguin Random House Children's
80 Strand, London WC2R 0RL

Photo credits

p.92. Warrior and Jack Seely, courtesy
of Isle of Wight Scout Council
p.92. Tirpitz, courtesy of Imperial War
Museums © IWM (Q 47559)
p.92. Rob, courtesy of Imperial War
Museums © IWM (HU 2618)
p.92. Chips, courtesy of Imperial War
Museums © IWM (TA 2635)
p.92. Simon, courtesy of Imperial War
Museums © IWM (HU 43656)
p.92. Wojtek, courtesy of Imperial War
Museums © IWM (HU 16546)
p.93. Jet, courtesy of Imperial War
Museums © IWM (FX 2901F)

p.93. Winkie, courtesy of Imperial War
Museums © IWM (HU 45623)
p.93. Winkie with trophy, courtesy of
Imperial War Museums © IWM
(HU 2892)
p.93. Joe, courtesy of Imperial War
Museums © IWM (HU 2899)
p.93. Lin Wang and Sun Li-jen, 1947,
unknown/Wikipedia.org
p.5 & 93. Antis, courtesy of Magdalena
Luscombe and Nina Buckley

p.93. K-Dog Dolphin, US Navy photo
by Photographers Mate 1st Class Brien
Aho. The appearance of US
Department of Defense (DoD) visual
information does not imply or
constitute DoD endorsement
p.93. Reckless, from the Randolph Pate
Collection (COLL/802) at the Archives
Branch, Marine Corps History
Division, Official USMC Photograph
p.93. Michael in suit with Roselle on
park bench, courtesy of Michael
Hingson

We have made every effort to locate the copyright holders for these images.
If there are any omissions/corrections to be made, please contact the publisher
so we can rectify this.

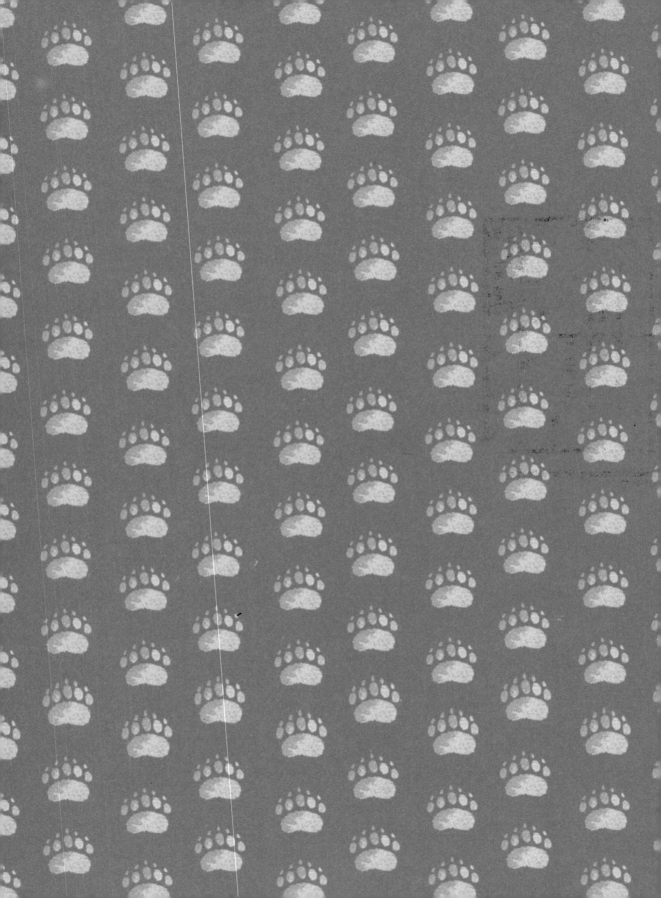